DRUG ADDICTION AND RECOVERY

Opioids: Heroin, OxyContin, and Painkillers

DRUG ADDICTION AND RECOVERY

Opioids: Heroin, OxyContin, and Painkillers

John Perritano

SERIES CONSULTANT
SARA BECKER, Ph.D.
Brown University School of Public Health
Warren Alpert Medical School

MASON CREST

Mason Crest
450 Parkway Drive, Suite D
Broomall, PA 19008
www.masoncrest.com

MTM Publishing, Inc.
www.mtmpublishing.com

President: Valerie Tomaselli
Vice President, Book Development: Hilary Poole
Designer: Annemarie Redmond
Copyeditor: Peter Jaskowiak
Editorial Assistant: Andrea St. Aubin

Series ISBN: 978-1-4222-3598-0
Hardback ISBN: 978-1-4222-3607-9
E-Book ISBN: 978-1-4222-8251-9

Cataloging-in-Publication Data on file with the Library of Congress

Printed and bound in the United States of America.

First printing
9 8 7 6 5 4 3 2 1

QR CODES AND LINKS TO THIRD PARTY CONTENT
You may gain access to certain third party content ("Third Party Sites") by scanning and using
the QR Codes that appear in this publication (the "QR Codes"). We do not operate or control in
any respect any information, products or services on such Third Party Sites linked to by us via
the QR Codes included in this publication and we assume no responsibility for any materials you
may access using the QR Codes. Your use of the QR Codes may be subject to terms, limitations,
or restrictions set forth in the applicable terms of use or otherwise established by the owners
of the Third Party Sites. Our linking to such Third Party Sites via the QR Codes does not imply an
endorsement or sponsorship of such Third Party Sites, or the information, products or services
offered on or through the Third Party Sites, nor does it imply an endorsement or sponsorship of this
publication by the owners of such Third Party Sites.

TABLE OF CONTENTS

Key Icons to Look for:

Words to Understand: These words with their easy-to-understand definitions will increase the reader's understanding of the text, while building vocabulary skills.

Sidebars: This boxed material within the main text allows readers to build knowledge, gain insights, explore possibilities, and broaden their perspectives by weaving together additional information to provide realistic and holistic perspectives.

Research Projects: Readers are pointed toward areas of further inquiry connected to each chapter. Suggestions are provided for projects that encourage deeper research and analysis.

Text-Dependent Questions: These questions send the reader back to the text for more careful attention to the evidence presented there.

Educational Videos: Readers can view videos by scanning our QR codes, providing them with additional educational content to supplement the text. Examples include news coverage, moments in history, speeches, iconic sports moments and much more!

Series Glossary of Key Terms: This back-of-the-book glossary contains terminology used throughout the series. Words found here increase the reader's ability to read and comprehend higher-level books and articles in this field.

SERIES INTRODUCTION

Many adolescents in the United States will experiment with alcohol or other drugs by time they finish high school. According to a 2014 study funded by the National Institute on Drug Abuse, about 27 percent of 8th graders have tried alcohol, 20 percent have tried drugs, and 13 percent have tried cigarettes. By 12th grade, these rates more than double: 66 percent of 12th graders have tried alcohol, 50 percent have tried drugs, and 35 percent have tried cigarettes.

Adolescents who use substances experience an increased risk of a wide range of negative consequences, including physical injury, family conflict, school truancy, legal problems, and sexually transmitted diseases. Higher rates of substance use are also associated with the leading causes of death in this age group: accidents, suicide, and violent crime. Relative to adults, adolescents who experiment with alcohol or other drugs progress more quickly to a full-blown substance use disorder and have more co-occurring mental health problems.

The National Survey on Drug Use and Health (NSDUH) estimated that in 2015 about 1.3 million adolescents between the ages of 12 and 17 (5 percent of adolescents in the United States) met the medical criteria for a substance use disorder. Unfortunately, the vast majority of these

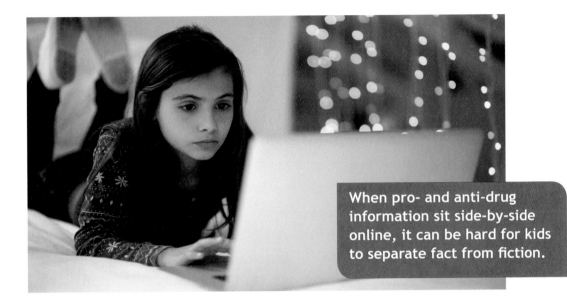

When pro- and anti-drug information sit side-by-side online, it can be hard for kids to separate fact from fiction.

adolescents did not receive treatment. Less than 10 percent of those with a diagnosis received specialty care, leaving 1.2 million adolescents with an unmet need for treatment.

The NSDUH asked the 1.2 million adolescents with untreated substance use disorders why they didn't receive specialty care. Over 95 percent said that they didn't think they needed it. The other 5 percent reported challenges finding quality treatment that was covered by their insurance. Very few treatment providers and agencies offer substance use treatment designed to meet the specific needs of adolescents. Meanwhile, numerous insurance plans have "opted out" of providing coverage for addiction treatment, while others have placed restrictions on what is covered.

Stigma about substance use is another serious problem. We don't call a person with an eating disorder a "food abuser," but we use terms like "drug abuser" to describe individuals with substance use disorders. Even treatment providers often unintentionally use judgmental words, such as describing urine screen results as either "clean" or "dirty." Underlying this language is the idea that a substance use disorder is some kind of moral failing or character flaw, and that people with these disorders deserve blame or punishment for their struggles.

And punish we do. A 2010 report by CASA Columbia found that in the United States, 65 percent of the 2.3 million people in prisons and jails met medical criteria for a substance use disorder, while another 20 percent had histories of substance use disorders, committed their crimes while under the influence of alcohol or drugs, or committed a substance-related crime. Many of these inmates spend decades in prison, but only 11 percent of them receive any treatment during their incarceration. Our society invests significantly more money in punishing individuals with substance use disorders than we do in treating them.

At a basic level, the ways our society approaches drugs and alcohol—declaring a "war on drugs," for example, or telling kids to "Just Say No!"—reflect a misunderstanding about the nature of addiction. The reality is that addiction is a disease that affects all types of people—parents and children, rich and poor, young and old. Substance use disorders stem from a complex interplay of genes, biology, and the environment, much like most physical and mental illnesses.

The way we talk about recovery, using phrases like "kick the habit" or "breaking free," also misses the mark. Substance use disorders are chronic, insidious, and debilitating illnesses. Fortunately, there are a number of effective treatments for substance use disorders. For many patients, however, the road is long and hard. Individuals recovering from substance use disorders can experience horrible withdrawal symptoms, and many will continue to struggle with cravings for alcohol or drugs. It can be a daily struggle to cope with these cravings and stay abstinent. A popular saying at Alcoholics Anonymous (AA) meetings is "one day at a time," because every day of recovery should be respected and celebrated.

There are a lot of incorrect stereotypes about individuals with substance use disorders, and there is a lot of false information about the substances, too. If you do an Internet search on the term "marijuana," for instance, two top hits are a web page by the National Institute on Drug Abuse and a page operated by Weedmaps, a medical and recreational marijuana dispensary. One of these pages publishes scientific information and one publishes pro-marijuana articles. Both pages have a high-quality, professional appearance. If you had never heard of either organization, it would be hard to know which to trust. It can be really difficult for the average person, much less the average teenager, to navigate these waters.

The topics covered in this series were specifically selected to be relevant to teenagers. About half of the volumes cover the types of drugs that they are most likely to hear about or to come in contact with. The other half cover important issues related to alcohol and other drug use (which we refer to as "drug use" in the titles for simplicity). These books cover topics such as the causes of drug use, the influence of drug use on the family, drug use and the legal system, drug use and mental health, and treatment options. Many teens will either have personal experience with these issues or will know someone who does.

This series was written to help young people get the facts about common drugs, substance use disorders, substance-related problems, and recovery. Accurate information can help adolescents to make better decisions. Students who are educated can help each other to better understand the risks and consequences of drug use. Facts also go a long way to reducing the stigma associated with substance use. We tend to fear or avoid things that we don't understand. Knowing the facts can make it easier to support each other. For students who know someone struggling with a substance use disorder, these books can also help them know what to expect. If they are worried about someone, or even about themselves, these books can help to provide some answers and a place to start.

—Sara J. Becker, Ph.D., Assistant Professor (Research), Center for Alcohol and Addictions Studies, Brown University School of Public Health, Assistant Professor (Research), Department of Psychiatry and Human Behavior, Brown University Medical School

WORDS TO UNDERSTAND

analgesic: pain-relieving substance.

apothecaries: drug stores.

endorphin: a natural painkiller in the body that attaches to the same cell receptors that morphine does.

hypodermic: a thin hollow needle used to inject substances under the skin.

laudanum: a solution of opium and alcohol once used to relieve pain.

synthesize: to chemically produce one substance from another.

synthetic: something that was produced artificially rather than derived from a natural substance.

tuberculosis: an infectious disease of the lungs.

CHAPTER ONE

OPIATES AND OPIOIDS

Deep in the Appalachian Mountains in Kentucky, where Pine Mountain and Cumberland Mountain meet, sits Bell County. For decades, the coal industry fueled the economy of this hardscrabble region. Eventually, however, the coal petered out, the mines shuttered, and the economy collapsed. Many people left the area to find work elsewhere. Unemployment rates were high, and in 2015 nearly two-thirds of adults did not have jobs. The median household income in 2013 was $25,228, and nearly 34 percent of Bell County's citizens were living in poverty.

Many people turned to drugs to lessen the pain that such difficulties can bring. The county's coroner, Jay Steele, witnessed many tragedies caused by drugs. He saw a little boy in diapers crying near the body of his great-grandfather, who had taken care of him because his addicted parents and grandparents could not. He also watched as the adult children of another man who had just passed away ran to the local pharmacy, hoping to refill their father's painkiller prescription to feed their addiction. "Day in and day out, you see the decline of people on drugs," Steele told *The Boston Globe*. "Some are just waiting to die."

OPIATE OVERLOAD

Opiates and opioids were the primary type of drug responsible for the tragedies in Bell County. Opiates are drugs **derived** from natural opium, which comes from the poppy plant. They include morphine, codeine, and most heroin. Opioids, on the other hand, are like opiates in their effects, but they are artificially made. OxyContin is an opioid. Some heroin is **synthetic**, and so is technically an opioid rather than an opiate. Due to all the overlap, the term *opioid* is also used as an umbrella term that can refer to both synthetic and naturally derived substances.

Seed pods of the opium poppy.

Unfortunately, what is happening in Bell County is mirrored in communities across the United States and around the world. During the past 20 years, an emerging opioid epidemic has caused politicians, police, doctors, and others to take notice. For example, the problem became so acute in Vermont that Governor Peter Shumlin

OPIOIDS BY THE NUMBERS

According to the American Society of Addiction Medicine, as of 2015:

- Opioid addiction occurs among all social and economic classes.
- Every single day, 46 Americans die from prescription opioid overdoses; that's roughly two deaths an hour, or nearly 17,000 each year.
- About 8,000 people die annually from overdosing on heroin.
- About three-quarters of those who misuse opioid painkillers eventually turn to heroin, because it is cheap to buy.
- One in 20 high school seniors has taken Vicodin.
- One in 30 high school seniors has misused OxyContin.

Source: American Society of Addiction Medicine, "Opioid Addiction Disease, 2015 Facts & Figures." http://www.asam.org/docs/default-source/advocacy/opioid-addiction-disease-facts-figures.pdf.

devoted his entire 2014 State of the State Address to what he said was a "full-blown heroin" crisis in Vermont. "In every corner of our state, heroin and opiate drug addiction threatens us," he said. "The time has come for us to stop quietly averting our eyes."

According to the United Nations Office on Drugs and Crime, an estimated 49 million people around the world misused opioids in 2012, the last year such numbers were available. In the United States, 2.1 million people suffer from a variety of medical disorders related to prescription opioid misuse.

One of the reasons for these staggering figures has been the burgeoning number of opioid prescriptions written by doctors since the early 1990s. In 1996, for example, U.S. doctors wrote enough OxyContin prescriptions to generate $48 million in sales—a modest figure. By 2002, however, sales for the drug hit $1.5 billion, and by 2010, sales reached $3.1 billion. The drug can vastly improve people's lives if used correctly. The problem comes when people take the drugs not as prescribed. In 2013 nearly 4.5 million Americans said they had used prescription painkillers within the last month, even though they had no medical reason to take the drugs.

HOW DO OPIOIDS AND OPIATES WORK?

People have been using and becoming addicted to opiates for centuries. Yet it wasn't until 1972 that researchers at Johns Hopkins University figured out how opiates worked and why the drugs are so addictive.

At that time, scientists discovered that human brain cells had a special receptor site that grabbed on to opioid drugs. They also discovered that morphine, the active ingredient in many synthetically derived opioids, had a chemical makeup similar to **endorphins**, natural

Opioids flood the brain with chemicals that are similar to—but much stronger than—the chemicals that are naturally released during physical activity.

chemicals created in the body that are responsible for feelings of happiness and well-being. When the body releases these natural "feel-good" chemicals, they flood the space between nerve cells creating a painkilling, or **analgesic**, effect. Endorphins can do a lot more than stop feelings of pain. They can make a person feel happy, even euphoric. Exercise and playing sports can release endorphins naturally.

Morphine acts the same way. It readily attaches itself to brain cells and overwhelms the receptor sites, creating an intense euphoric and painkilling sensation. Morphine is much stronger then endorphins, and the more morphine there is in a person's body, the more exhilarated that person feels. The euphoria created by morphine is why opioids are highly addictive.

OPIOIDS AND OPIATES: A SHORT HISTORY

Opium is unlike any other drug. Nations and civilizations built trade routes to make sure people's thirst for opium was quenched. Countries even went to war over opium. Opium's raw material, the poppy plant, was first cultivated by the ancient Sumerians some 5,000 years ago. The Sumerians lived in southern Mesopotamia and called the poppy the "joy plant" because of its mind-altering effects. Inside the poppy seed is a gum—opium. Workers tap the gum from inside the seeds by slicing the pods open with a knife. They then allow the gum to dry until it solidifies into a putty-like material. It can then be beaten or rolled into cakes or blocks.

The cultivation and harvesting of the poppy, and the production of opium, spread over time across the ancient world into Asia, Europe, and, later, North America. People around the world have smoked opium or eaten or drank opium mixtures for recreational use.

Opium also has a long history of being used for medicinal purposes. Doctors gave it to patients to deaden the pain of surgery or a broken

At the turn of the last century, there were many products available containing opium that anyone could buy.

leg. Beginning in the 1600s, one of the most popular opium-based medicines was laudanum, a compound originally created from opium, sherry wine, and herbs. Doctors prescribed laudanum for various ailments, including headaches and tuberculosis, a debilitating lung disease.

In the early 1800s, a pharmacist's assistant named Friedrich Wilhelm Sertürner discovered morphine—a yellowish-white crystal compound—after immersing opium in a solution of hot water and ammonia. He tested the compound on himself and found that it reduced pain and created a feeling of euphoria. He named the new drug after Morpheus, the Greek god of dreams. Morphine turned out to be more powerful than opium, and doctors started giving it to their patients because of its intense painkilling qualities. What they didn't know was that morphine was even more addictive than opium.

Companies soon put morphine derivatives into cough syrups, elixirs, and a variety of concoctions marketed as "cure-alls." One of the most famous examples was "Mrs. Winslow's Soothing Syrup," which was marketed as a way to calm fussy infants dealing with teething pain and contained a whopping 65 milligrams of morphine per ounce. Another popular concoction was "Dr. McNunn's Elixir of Opium," which was touted as a safe, "nonhabit-forming" version of opium to treat convulsions, pain, irritability, and nervous excitement in both adults and children. But McNunn's Elixir caused a rash of infant deaths before it was finally pulled from the market. All of these treatments, and more, could be legally purchased at local apothecaries or through the mail.

When the hypodermic needle was perfected in 1853, both medicinal and recreational morphine use ballooned. Doctors used the drug with great success during the U.S. Civil War (1861–1865) to treat wounded soldiers. However, those who survived their wounds often became addicted to the

drug. About two decades after the war, a chemist learned how to synthesize heroin from morphine. The scientist, however, thought the drug a bust, and threw what he had created in the trash. But about a decade later, in 1898, a German company named Bayer used this scientist's research to begin marketing its own version of heroin. Bayer advertised the drug as a "nonaddictive" morphine

Corporal Michael Dunn of the Pennsylvania Infantry lost both his legs in a battle in Georgia, in 1864. Morphine would have been one of the few medicines available to help him survive.

substitute. The company put it in cough syrup and doctors used it treat morphine and opium addiction.

In later years, other synthetic opioids became widely available as painkillers, including Vicodin, OxyContin (covered in next chapter), and codeine. That's when the real crisis began.

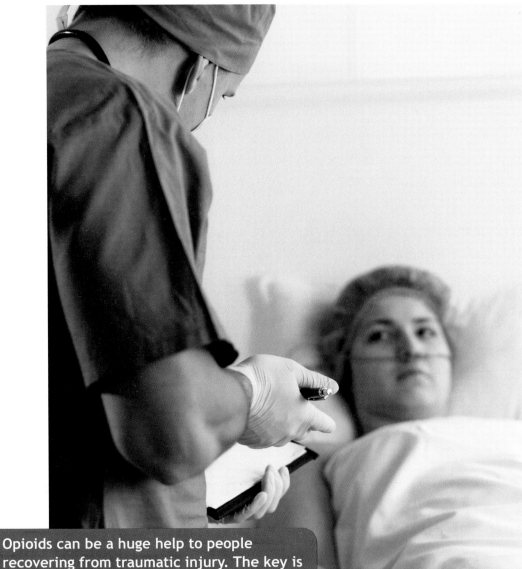

Opioids can be a huge help to people recovering from traumatic injury. The key is to use them only as directed by a physician.

DEPENDENCE AND ADDICTION

In 2012, doctors wrote 259 million opioid pain medication prescriptions, enough for every adult in the United States to have a bottle for themselves. The result has been a spike in addiction and dependency.

Addiction and dependency are two separate things. *Addiction* is characterized by an inability to stop using a drug. The mind craves the drug's effects. As a result, using and getting the drug becomes central to the addict's life. An addict may fail to meet family, social, or work obligations. In severe cases, the addict may lie to people or manipulate them, or may even commit crimes to obtain the drug.

A person becomes *dependent* on a drug when his or her body develops a tolerance to it. As the body adapts, it requires more of the drug to achieve the same effects. Physical dependency can develop with chronic use of prescription opioids. It can also develop when the drugs are taken as recommended by a doctor. However, just because a person is physically dependent on a drug does not mean that person is an addict, although the two often go hand-in-hand.

When a dependent person stops using the drug, he or she will often have withdrawal symptoms as the level of the drug in the body decreases. A person might sweat profusely, shake, or have difficulty breathing, or the person might hallucinate.

SOCCER MOM ADDICT

Candace, a mother of two, is a textbook example of a person both dependent on and addicted to opioids. She was in a car crash that broke her neck and left her temporarily paralyzed and in a lot of pain. Doctors prescribed OxyContin to lessen her suffering. The pills were a godsend. OxyContin helped alleviate much of the discomfort Candace was feeling. Her neck eventually healed, but her pain never fully subsided. Eventually,

Candace became dependent on the drug. She took higher and higher doses to relieve the pain. Over time, she became addicted. She now craved the drug—not only for its painkilling properties, but also for the way it made her feel emotionally.

After a while, she lost her health insurance and access to the pills. She started buying OxyContin illegally on the street, but that became too expensive. As has happened to so many people, Candace then found a painkiller that was cheaper: heroin. She started snorting it though her nose a few times a week. Soon she craved more, and she started using it daily. After a few months, Candace began injecting the drug into her veins.

Candace was not a stereotypical opioid addict. She cared for her kids, ran the house, and held down a job. She even took care of her grandmother. No one, not a soul, knew about her addiction. Candace told the *Daily Beast*, an online news site in the United States, that she felt ashamed her addiction and dependency on opioids had gotten so out of control. While she had blended seamlessly into society, going to book clubs and PTA meetings, the tracks of heroin use on her arms remained hidden.

Candace's story demonstrates that people who have issues with opioids aren't always the stereotypical "drug addicts" portrayed in the media.

"I don't know where to go for help or how to even begin. I want to stop though, but I know I can't do it on my own because I've tried," she wrote in an email to the *Daily Beast*. "I'm honestly just tired of waking up . . . believing wholeheartedly that maybe, just maybe, my two boys would have a better life in a different situation, possibly if it were one in which I wasn't in it."

TEXT-DEPENDENT QUESTIONS

1. Name three types of opioids.
2. How many people are estimated to be abusing opioids around the world?
3. Which invention caused morphine addiction to increase?

RESEARCH PROJECT

Use a computer to print out a line map of the world. Next, gather information on the top five opium-producing and top five opium-consuming countries. Shade in each of the countries with a different color: one color for the producer nations, another for the consumer nations. What can you conclude about this map? (You might look for data at the websites of the United Nations Office on Drugs and Crime [http://www.unodc.org/wdr2014/en/opiates.html] and the CIA's World Factbook [https://www.cia.gov/library/publications/the-world-factbook/fields/2086.html].)

WORDS TO UNDERSTAND

biochemist: scientist who studies the chemistry of living organisms.

cellulitis: a bacterial infection of the skin and the tissues beneath the skin.

dilute: adding water to another liquid in order to make that liquid thinner and weaker in strength.

hepatitis: a disease of the liver causing abdominal pain, weakness, and a yellowing of the skin.

inhibitions: feelings that prevent someone from behaving spontaneously.

molecule: a chemical compound consisting of one or more atoms.

respiration: breathing.

urination: process by which the body expels wastewater, also known as urine.

CHAPTER TWO

HEROIN

He keeps a long shirt on in the middle of summer to hide the needle marks. It's been 11 days since "Bill" (a fake name, used to protect his identity) has injected himself with heroin. As he tells his story to a reporter, Bill is undergoing an intense physical withdrawal. He fidgets. He shakes. He sweats. Eleven days without a fix is a long time for a heroin addict. Bill's been down this road before, though. "It's been on and off for a long time," he tells the reporter. "I get clean, I go back to it. I get clean. I go back to it. . . . It's a vicious cycle."

Bill has played a heavy price for his addiction. He has shared needles with other users and contracted **hepatitis** C, a dangerous and highly infectious disease. He's gotten infections such as **cellulitis**, which, if left untreated, can kill. He has personally overdosed twice and taken three friends to the hospital, when they overdosed in his presence.

Bill first began using drugs when he was 14. He had a history of mental health problems and had spent some of his early teen years in residential treatment. At the age of 14, he started experimenting with alcohol, marijuana, and some of the drugs he'd been prescribed for his mental health treatment. He also experimented with Vicodin, a painkiller

Heroin in close-up.

that contains an opiate derivative called hydrocodone, and found that he liked how it made him feel. Bill later graduated from Vicodin to the much stronger OxyContin.

Heroin was next for Bill. First he snorted it, then he injected it. "Everyone was saying it was just like doing Oxy and it's cheaper. Oxy is $60 for an 8-milligram pill. You're spending $20 (on heroin) and you're getting the same high." At first, the heroin helped Bill to feel calm and to "numb everything" out. Still, the drug was slowly eating away at his body and mind. "You don't think about any problems you have going on. When you're high, nothing bothers you anymore."

A FAMILIAR STORY

Any other heroin user can relate to Bill's story. Heroin use has spiraled out of control in the United States since the mid 1990s. According to the latest numbers from the Centers for Disease Control and Prevention (CDC), there were 8,260 heroin-related deaths in 2013. That was 2,333 more than in 2012. It was the third year in a row that heroin deaths increased.

In Bill's hometown of Bay City, Michigan, police and local officials say the community of just over 34,000 people is in the throes of a heroin epidemic. In the first six months of 2015, 20 people had to be taken to the emergency room to be treated for heroin overdoses. The problem got so bad that the county's health department issued an advisory outlining ways to combat the situation. The National Institute on Drug Abuse (NIDA) says that half of all young people today who use heroin misused prescription opioids first. This is clearly not what C. R. Alder Wright, the developer of heroin, had intended.

THE BEGINNINGS OF HEROIN

The year was 1874, and Wright, a British chemist, was about to turn the drug world on its ear, although no one knew it at the time. Bearded and dapper, Wright discovered heroin after boiling morphine with a chemical compound with the unwieldy name of acetic anhydride, which is now used to make aspirin.

Wright, who worked at St. Mary's Hospital in Paddington, England, was trying to find a derivative of morphine that was not habit forming. He fed the grayish powder to his dog to see what would happen. The dog died. Wright threw the rest of his concoction into the trash, but he did publish an article about how he had made the substance.

No one gave Wright's discovery a second thought for two decades. In 1898, the Bayer drug company in Germany resurrected Wright's discovery and began making its own batch of his drug. Chemists at the company tested it on rats and rabbits, which responded well to the drug. It was then tested on humans. The drug suppressed their coughing fits. The patients also liked it, and they wanted more. One called it *heroisch*, which in English means "heroic." Heroin finally had a name.

Bayer's scientists took the powder they made and stuffed it into capsules. They **diluted** it in liquids and sold it as a general cure for chest

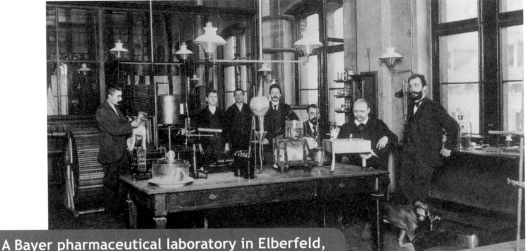

A Bayer pharmaceutical laboratory in Elberfeld, Germany, in the late 19th century.

pain, pneumonia, and tuberculosis. Users could drink, swallow, or inject the drug. One advertisement stated, "HEROIN-HYDROCHLORIDE is preeminently adapted for the manufacture of cough elixirs, cough balsams, cough drops . . . and cough medicines of any kind . . . it is the CHEAPEST SPECIFIC FOR THE RELIEF OF COUGHS." The price was $4.85 per ounce, "less in larger quantities." The company produced 1 ton of heroin during the first year of production. By the early 1900s, it was sold in 23 countries.

Unaware of heroin's addictive qualities, doctors used the drug liberally to treat those addicted to cocaine and opium. Eventually, the eyes of the medical community were opened to the seriousness of heroin. But although some doctors labeled heroin as an addictive drug, others ignored the warnings and continued to dispense it to their patients. "I feel that bringing charges against heroin is almost like questioning the fidelity of a good friend," wrote one doctor in the *Kentucky Medical Journal*. "I have used it with good results."

By 1925, there were 200,000 heroin addicts in the United States. As of 2015, about 4.2 million Americans aged 12 and older have used heroin at least once in their lives. Experts say that 23 percent of those who use heroin become dependent on the drug. In fact, heroin is the most addictive of all opioids, and perhaps of all drugs.

HOW HEROIN WORKS

A person can administer heroin in several ways. The drug can be snorted, smoked, inhaled, or injected. All of these methods will deliver the drug into the bloodstream, which sends it rapidly through the body. If heroin is injected, it takes about 30 seconds to work its way through the body, moving through the bloodstream to organs and the brain. The drug finds its way to the central nervous system, creating a sense of well-being and euphoria. As it moves inside the body, a person's respiration slows. The skin

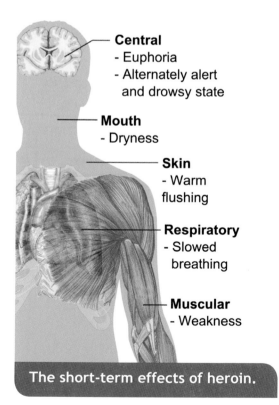

Central
- Euphoria
- Alternately alert
  and drowsy state

Mouth
- Dryness

Skin
- Warm
  flushing

Respiratory
- Slowed
  breathing

Muscular
- Weakness

The short-term effects of heroin.

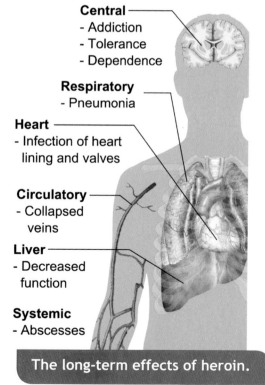

Central
- Addiction
- Tolerance
- Dependence

Respiratory
- Pneumonia

Heart
- Infection of heart
  lining and valves

Circulatory
- Collapsed
  veins

Liver
- Decreased
  function

Systemic
- Abscesses

The long-term effects of heroin.

HEROIN'S SIDE EFFECTS

The following is a list of the impacts of long-term heroin use:

- relaxed muscles
- bad teeth
- constipation
- itching
- cold sweats
- weakened immune system
- reduced sexual desire
- loss of memory
- depression
- sleeplessness
- loss of appetite

begins to flush and feel warm. Urination becomes difficult. A strong dose can make a person vomit.

Once molecules of morphine reach the brain, they attach to the opioid receptors on cells, including those associated with perceptions of pain and reward. Morphine also attaches to cells in the brain stem, which controls many life processes. A person can become addicted to heroin amazingly fast. The brain will send signals to the rest of the body, asking it to send more morphine into the bloodstream. Over time, a person develops a

NICKNAMES

Heroin goes by many names, including the following:

- big H
- black pearl
- black tar
- brown crystal
- brown sugar
- chiba
- China white
- chiva
- dope
- dragon (smoking heroin is called "chasing the dragon")
- H
- horse
- junk
- Mexican mud
- nod
- scag
- smack
- snowball
- tar
- white
- white lady

physical tolerance to the drug, and the brain will need larger doses to achieve the same state of euphoria created by the morphine.

Euphoria can manifest itself in several ways. First the person feels a "rush." This feeling lasts a minute or two, and the user might feel slightly dizzy. When the rush dissipates, the high kicks in, lasting for hours as the morphine diffuses from the bloodstream into the brain. Addicts describe a sense of satisfaction and drowsiness. It doesn't take long for a person to start craving the drug.

THE HORRORS OF WITHDRAWAL

"Eight to twelve hours after the last dose the addict begins to grow uneasy. A sense of weakness overcomes him, he yawns, shivers and sweats all at the same time. . . . Now, to add further to the addict's miseries, his bowels begin to act with fantastic violence: great waves of contractions pass over the stomach, causing explosive vomiting. . . . As many as sixty large watery stools may be passed in twenty-four hours."

Once the body has become accustomed to regular doses of opioids, going without them becomes extremely unpleasant and even dangerous.

MANY DANGERS

People who inject heroin often suffer from a variety of diseases including HIV/AIDS and hepatitis C. Both are transmitted through contact with bodily fluids, which can be transferred from sharing needles. HIV is short for "human immunodeficiency virus." Unlike other viruses, the body's immune system cannot kill HIV. It can lead to full-blown AIDS (acquired immunodeficiency syndrome), which puts a person at very high risk for many other infections.

Hepatitis C is a liver disease, and it is also caused by a virus. It can be a serious and lifelong illness. People can also contract a number of sexually transmitted diseases because heroin use reduces **inhibitions** and makes it more likely that two people will have unprotected sex.

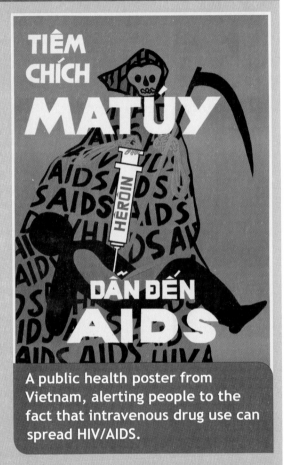

A public health poster from Vietnam, alerting people to the fact that intravenous drug use can spread HIV/AIDS.

The **biochemist** and author Robert S. de Ropp wrote plainly, if somewhat squeamishly, in 1958, describing what happens to a heroin addict when he stops using the drug. De Ropp's book, *Drugs and the Mind*, underscores the drug's addictive quantities by the severity of withdrawal.

One dose of heroin can create a euphoric feeling that can last for four to six hours, but detoxifying from that same dose can take about a week.

Habitual users go through the most severe withdrawals. "Twenty-four to thirty-six hours after his last dose the addict presents a truly dreadful spectacle," de Ropp wrote. "He covers himself with every blanket he can find. His whole body is shaken by twitching. . . . Throughout this period the addict obtains neither sleep nor rest."

HEROIN IN SUBURBIA

Not that long ago, heroin was the scourge of urban neighborhoods—its reputation was of a cheap drug that only the poor used. This is no longer the case. Today, the people who use heroin the most are young, white, and live in affluent suburbs. Their path to heroin addiction most likely began with the misuse of prescription painkillers.

A survey of 9,000 patients at drug treatment centers around the country published in 2014 by the journal *JAMA Psychiatry* found that 90 percent of heroin users were, on average, 23 years old. Most began abusing heroin after using other prescription opioids. By comparison, in the 1960s and 1970s, most heroin users were young, poor, minority men who lived in the inner city.

Problems with heroin are not limited to "bad" neighborhoods. The heroin epidemic is affecting all kinds of people.

Most people need help as they get off the drug. Many heroin addicts will take a synthetic opioid called methadone (discussed further in chapter four) to kick their heroin addiction. Methadone reduces the symptoms of withdrawal without causing euphoric feelings. But methadone can itself be addictive if not used correctly.

THE PSYCHOLOGY OF AN ADDICT

Whether a person lives on the streets of Philadelphia or in a quaint Vermont town, heroin addiction has a unique psychology apart from other drugs. Reasons vary for why a person begins using the drug. For some, it is a way to self-medicate to deal with issues such as depression and anxiety. Others use heroin because they lack self-esteem. Still others might have been abused as a child, and the use of the drug is a way to build a wall between them and harsh memories. Some addicts may feel lonely and inferior and believe they cannot keep up with the rest of society.

Once heroin use begins, however, researchers say the drug provides a way for some people to develop a social network, one that makes life a bit easier to bear. Some addicts will hang out together trying to score a baggie or two of the drug. As they wait, they might talk about the day's events

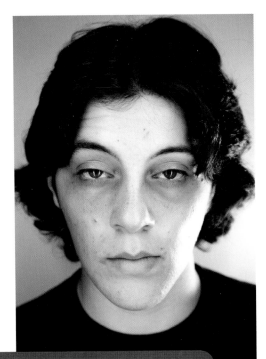

The sleepy state associated with heroin use is called "nodding."

or people they know. Or they may involve one another in their rituals of using and getting high. Some heroin users share needles. They do it in part because they want to get high, but they also share needles as a way to connect with one another.

"The heroin culture provides a social identity for its members," writes Humberto Fernandez and Therissa A. Libby, in their book *Heroin: Its History, Pharmacology, and Treatment*. "A heroin addict can feel disenfranchised, lonely, inferior, and incapable of competing with the rest of society. . . . Perhaps the desperate nature and magnitude of the need to connect with another human being—a need so powerful one would risk one's life for it— speaks to the levels of pain and emptiness heroin addicts experience."

TEXT-DEPENDENT QUESTIONS

1. How many heroin-related deaths were there in 2013?
2. Which illnesses did Bayer claim heroin could cure?
3. What are some of the physical effects that heroin can have on a person during withdrawal?

RESEARCH PROJECT

Research and create a list of drug treatment centers in your community. Once you have done that, create a public awareness poster that can help people who might be seeking treatment.

WORDS TO UNDERSTAND

acetaminophen: drug that relieves pain and reduces fever, usually bought in low doses over the counter.

clustered: grouped together in a small area.

irritable: easily annoyed.

neonatal: related to a newborn child, one who is less than a month old.

CHAPTER THREE

OXYCONTIN

Cathy Pederson, her gun and handcuffs hidden, is a cop in Norfolk, Virginia. She's looking for drug dealers and users, but her beat isn't a city neighborhood—it's the local drugstore. She's not looking for bags of heroin or crack, but for those illegally buying and selling painkilling prescription drugs.

Many of those she will arrest have dropped off forged prescriptions, a felony that can lead to some serious jail time. The criminals come from all walks of life: grandmothers, teenage girls, lawyers, and teachers. All are caught in an epidemic that is spiraling out of control—addiction to opioids including Vicodin, Percocet, and, most of all, OxyContin.

"They didn't meet opiates at a party," Penderson tells a reporter. "They didn't start taking them for fun. There's usually a car accident or a surgery somewhere in their background, and they became addicted to their pain meds." Pederson also busts the drug dealers who make a living selling prescription opioids. It's a tale that can be told in every state, city, town, and village across America.

OVERPRESCRIBED

Of all the opioid painkillers, OxyContin is among the most misused in the country. It is also one of the newest. Approved by the U.S. Food and Drug Administration in 1995, OxyContin is derived from an opioid called oxycodone, which German scientists developed in 1916. The drug arrived in the United States 20 years later.

In 1995 the drug company Purdue Pharma, based in Stamford, Connecticut, began producing and marketing OxyContin. Within seven years, the drug became the best-selling painkiller in the country. It was described as a miracle pill, just as heroin was nearly a century before. OxyContin is an effective painkiller because it is time released; that is, it enters the bloodstream slowly. When used properly, the drug can provide a person with 12 hours of pain relief, four times more than non-opioid painkillers such as aspirin or acetaminophen.

Like other opioids, oxycodone stimulates certain opioid receptors in the brain and spinal cord. While its analgesic effect is extremely effective, the drug can also create a sense of euphoria, which is why OxyContin can be dangerously addictive. At first, doctors prescribed OxyContin to cancer patients to manage their chronic pain. It didn't take long for physicians to prescribe the pills to others. By 2010, the United States was consuming 80

Many people depend on prescription opiates for pain relief.

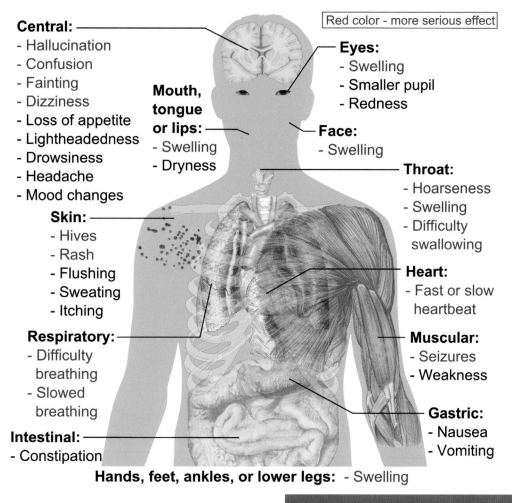

Red color - more serious effect

Central:
- Hallucination
- Confusion
- Fainting
- Dizziness
- Loss of appetite
- Lightheadedness
- Drowsiness
- Headache
- Mood changes

Mouth, tongue or lips:
- Swelling
- Dryness

Eyes:
- Swelling
- Smaller pupil
- Redness

Face:
- Swelling

Throat:
- Hoarseness
- Swelling
- Difficulty swallowing

Skin:
- Hives
- Rash
- Flushing
- Sweating
- Itching

Heart:
- Fast or slow heartbeat

Respiratory:
- Difficulty breathing
- Slowed breathing

Muscular:
- Seizures
- Weakness

Intestinal:
- Constipation

Gastric:
- Nausea
- Vomiting

Hands, feet, ankles, or lower legs: - Swelling

Oxycodone is a powerful drug that can have many side effects.

percent of the world's oxycodone, the active ingredient in OxyContin and Percocet. As the number of OxyContin prescriptions increased, the number of OxyContin overdose deaths surged. The more people used the drug, they more they became addicted.

Americans weren't the only ones misusing OxyContin. In Canada, the use of the drug and other opioids became the leading cause of death in young people. One out of every eight deaths in Canada over a period of 20

MORE THAN PHYSICAL

The physical effects of oxycodone are noted in the image on page 37. But it can also cause depression, anxiety, irritability, and mood swings. Dependency on opioids can also inspire behaviors such as lying, forging prescriptions, borrowing or stealing money, and neglecting responsibilities at work or at school.

years was related to opioid overdoses. In Ontario, the opioid death rate between 1991 and 2010 rose from 12.7 deaths per million to 41.6 deaths per million, or roughly 550 people each year, a staggering increase of 242 percent. Researchers said OxyContin and hydrocodone pills were the most frequently misused opioid pain killers in Canada.

MARKETING

Many people have wondered how the drug OxyContin came to be so widely misused in such a short time. Some of the blame has fallen on physicians for overprescribing the drug, and even more on Purdue, the drug company that marketed the drug. Pharmaceutical companies invest a lot of money in advertising their products to doctors. As often happens, Purdue heavily marketed OxyContin to doctors in the hopes they would write more prescriptions.

To do this, the company created profiles for doctors, which documented what types of drugs each physician prescribed. Using these profiles, the company identified the doctors who wrote the most and least amount of prescriptions in each community. Purdue was particularly interested in finding doctors that routinely prescribed large quantities of opioids, which would tell the company which physicians treated the largest numbers of patients with chronic-pain ailments.

The company's sales reps used this and other information to push OxyContin, especially among doctors that prescribed high numbers of opioids. The company also increased its sales force, and gave first-time customers a free prescription coupon for a 7 to 30-day supply of the drug. By 2001, customers had used nearly 34,000 coupons.

The company also marketed the drug for "nonmalignant" pain— defined as pain symptoms lasting three months or more. This grew the OxyContin market considerably. This new market eventually constituted 86 percent of all opioid sales in 1999, researchers say. The result was a 10-fold increase in OxyContin prescriptions, from 670,000 in 1997 to about 6.2 million in 2002.

As was the case with other formulations of opiates and morphine derivatives, the researchers say the company also downplayed the addictive quality of the medicine. "A consistent feature in the promotion and marketing of OxyContin was a systematic effort to minimize the risk of addiction in the use of opioids for the treatment of chronic noncancer-related pain," wrote Dr. Art Van Zee in the *American Journal of Public Health*. When people asked about the risk

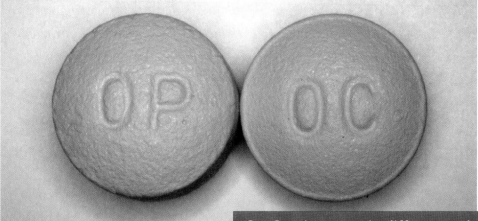

OxyContin comes in different-colored tablets depending on how strong it is. These two are 20-milligram doses.

A DOWNWARD SPIRAL

Evidence suggests that as the misuse of prescription opioids decreases, heroin use increases. The National Institute of Drug Abuse compared data on the percentage of people in the United States using opioids from the start of 2009 through the end of 2012. They found that while the percentage of prescription opioid misuse was still high, it was on the downswing. But it was mirrored by a rise in the use of heroin.

for addiction, Van Zee said, "Purdue trained its sales representatives to carry the message that the risk of addiction was "less than 1 percent." Yet unlike the marketing of early opiates and morphine derivatives, which often reflected a lack of understanding about the addictive properties, there is evidence to suggest that the marketing of OxyContin was intentionally deceptive.

In 2007, Purdue Pharma and three of its top executives pled guilty to criminal charges that they misled the U.S. Food and Drug Administration (FDA), clinicians, and patients about the risks of OxyContin addiction by aggressively marketing the drug to providers and patients as a safe alternative to shorter-acting opioids.

By the late 2000s, people finally began waking up to the realities of OxyContin misuse. Communities were being ravaged by the drug. Some states took action. Kentucky took Purdue to court, claiming bad behavior ranging from false advertising to fraud, because OxyContin misuse had become a major problem in that state. The addictive qualities of the drug were brought to light in other lawsuits, which resulted in Purdue being ordered to pay stiff fines. Despite this, the family that owns the firm was singled out as one of the world's richest families in 2015.

HOW DOES OXYCONTIN WORK?

Those who misuse OxyContin can swallow or chew the pills. Some also crush them and snort them. Others who want an intense and instant "high" will pulverize the drug, cook it in water with a spoon and lighter, and inject it into their veins. Although a person needs a doctor's prescription to purchase the drug, it is widely available through illicit channels. Dealers sell the drug on the street. Some people steal the drug from medicine cabinets of friends and relatives. Others forge prescriptions. Still others will get the drug by convincing doctors they have symptoms that they really don't have.

A 2014 study in the journal *Medical Care* concluded that patients can influence their doctor's prescribing habits. The study's authors used professional actors and had them visit 192 primary care physicians in six states. Each of the "patients" feigned symptoms of back pain. Half of the "actors" specifically asked the doctor for oxycodone, while the other half did not. About 20 percent of the actors that requested the drug received

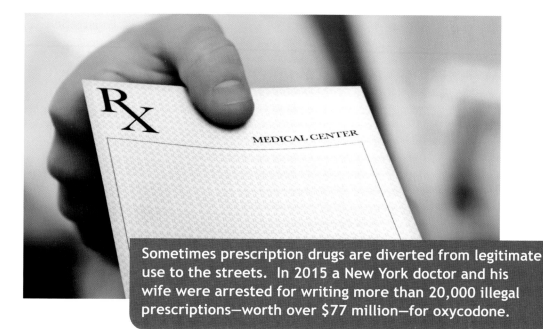

Sometimes prescription drugs are diverted from legitimate use to the streets. In 2015 a New York doctor and his wife were arrested for writing more than 20,000 illegal prescriptions—worth over $77 million—for oxycodone.

it. Only 1 percent who didn't ask for oxycodone received a prescription. However, 73 percent of the doctors who did not write scripts for oxycodone prescribed stronger narcotics to the patients who asked for oxycodone.

Over the last several years, drug companies have been trying to crack down on OxyContin misuse by making the pills harder to crush. As a result, those addicted to OxyContin have found the pills harder and more expensive to get. The cost of an 80-milligram OxyContin pill can range from $60 to $100. As the cost has grown, and as these tighter restrictions have been put in place, experts have seen prescription-painkiller misuse decrease, especially among adults 18 to 25. However, that drop has been paired with a rise in heroin misuse. Heroin is much cheaper to buy than OxyContin, costing roughly $10 for a small baggie of the powder.

In 2012 nearly 30 percent of those who responded to a survey by the National Institute on Drug Abuse misused oxycodone, down from nearly 48 percent in 2009. During the same period, however, heroin use increased from 10 percent in 2009 to 20 percent in 2012. "One substance will go down, but another will go up," Ronni Katz, a substance abuse prevention program coordinate in Portland, Maine, told *USA Today*.

NEONATAL ABSTINENCE SYNDROME

It was the middle of the night in Bangor, Maine, when the hospital called. Tonya picked the phone up and learned that her three-day-old baby boy was showing signs of opioid withdrawal. Doctors were going to give the baby methadone, the drug heroin addicts use to ease their withdrawal symptoms. It didn't come as a shock to Tonya or to the doctors or nurses. Tonya had been abusing OxyContin for the first 12 weeks of her pregnancy. She bought the drug on the street and then turned to daily doses of methadone to wean herself off the drug and manage her withdrawal symptoms.

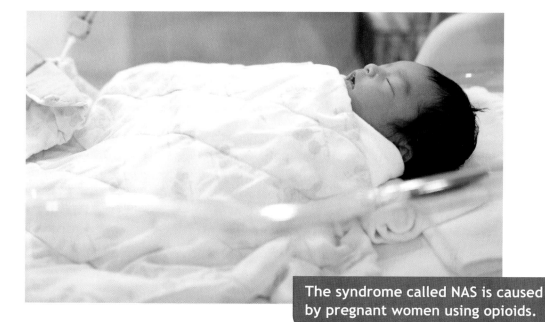

The syndrome called NAS is caused by pregnant women using opioids.

For several years now, doctors and nurses have been dealing with a new and potentially deadly challenge: getting newborns off opioid painkillers. Many of the children have to stay in the hospital for weeks as doctors and nurses try to wean them off the drugs. The condition is called **neonatal** abstinence syndrome, or NAS for short. Children suffering from NAS cry nonstop. They jerk their tiny heads, feet, and legs just like an addict coming down from a high. The children vomit and have such intense diarrhea that it burns the skin off their bottoms.

Ironically, the babies are treated with the same opioids that got them in such a sorry state. What the future holds for babies born addicted to OxyContin is a mystery. No one knows how each child will develop or what problems it might have as it gets older. Moreover, exact numbers describing the extent of the problem are elusive. One study, conducted between 2000 and 2009 and published in the *Journal of the American Medical Association*, said more than 13,000 newborns were diagnosed with the condition during that 10-year period.

The crisis has occurred in part because doctors were handing out opioid prescriptions to pregnant women at an alarming rate—14 percent just in the United States. The misuse of these prescription pain relievers resulted in a 300 percent increase of NAS between 2000 and 2009. More recent data released from hospitals suggests that the rates of NAS secondary to opioid addiction continue to rise. Hospitals in Kentucky and West Virginia, where opioid misuse is rampant, have reported a steep rise in the number of NAS children. In Florida, several counties **clustered** around Tampa Bay, reported that 30 percent of babies in the neonatal intensive care unit suffer from opioid withdrawal.

OXY FOR THE YOUNG

In 2015 the FDA approved the use of OxyContin for children as young as 11, drawing a storm of criticism from those who fear that the children could

The approval of oxycodone for young kids was met with a great deal of criticism from those who worry about introducing such a powerful opiate to people who are so young.

be put at risk for addiction. The FDA said children have few options when it comes to pain relief. The agency asked Purdue to study whether the drug could be used safely by children ages 11 to 16 who suffer chronic pain from cancer, severe trauma, or surgery.

However, some doctors say that prescribing OxyContin to children so young could lead them down the path of drug addiction. Teenagers are especially vulnerable because their brains have yet to fully mature. Over half a million people 12 years or older use OxyContin for nonmedical reasons, and 1 in 30 high school seniors misuse the drug. "Among adolescents who are prescribed OxyContin, a small but significant number are going to become addicted," Scott Hadland, from Boston Children's Hospital and Harvard Medical School, told *USA Today*.

TEXT-DEPENDENT QUESTIONS

1. Name three side effects of OxyContin abuse.
2. What is the active ingredient in OxyContin?
3. Why is OxyContin an effective painkiller?

RESEARCH PROJECT

Research and write a report on how Purdue, the makers of OxyContin, marketed the painkilling pills to doctors. You can use the Internet and the library to research news accounts of the company's practices. Make sure you include the outcome of legal cases, as well as the impact the availability of the drug had on specific communities who criticized the company.

WORDS TO UNDERSTAND

administer: give medication to someone.

inpatient: a person who stays at a hospital or other medical facility and receives treatment.

psychiatric: relating to mental illness or its treatment.

psychotherapy: the treatment of mental disorders by talking with a mental health professional.

CHAPTER FOUR

TREATMENT

Patrick Cagey walked out of treatment looking fit, spry, and in great health. It had only taken 30 days. At 25, Patrick had his life back together. He expected to find a job and maybe enroll in graduate school. His future, as they say, was bright. After walking out of rehab, he visited a childhood friend who had become a shut-in. He went to the gym. He apologized to his girlfriend. "It was the most wonderful conversation we had," she said. "I said, 'Everything's going to be OK. You keep talking this way, I'll marry you tomorrow.'"

A few days later, four days after leaving rehab, Patrick was dead, the victim of a heroin overdose. Patrick's story, chronicled in the *Huffington Post*, is a vivid reminder that even when an opioid addict wants help, gets treatment, and seemingly survives the worst the drug can offer, the situation can go downhill quickly. Patrick seemed to have taken responsibility for his addiction. He attended Narcotic Anonymous (NA) meetings. But old habits die hard. When his parents could not get in touch with Patrick, his father went to his son's house. He let himself inside and checked the bathroom, only to find his son's body. On the kitchen counter were the tools of his demons: a spoon, a cotton ball, a lighter, and a cap to a syringe.

According to the National Institute on Drug Abuse, nearly 5 percent of admissions to publicly funded treatment programs are people who misuse opioids, not including heroin. The percentage of admissions for heroin users is 14.1 percent.

DETOXIFICATION

The first step toward treatment is a conscious decision by a person to seek treatment. That decision is often forced upon the person by family and friends concerned about her or his health and well-being, or the legal system that may mandate treatment. Once the decision to seek treatment has been made, the next step is to detoxify, or rid the body of the drug. Detoxification should be done in a controlled setting under the watchful eye of doctors and nurses. As the body detoxifies, a series of physical withdrawal symptoms typically begin to emerge. A person may become agitated, and he or she may sweat, shake, vomit, and have diarrhea.

Detoxifying from heroin and other opioids can go on for hours, and sometimes days. It can be torturous. Dr. Marc Myer, who helps treat patients while they are in detox, knows all too well the effects of heroin detoxification. He has a personal history of opioid addiction, and his

EXPENSIVE CARE

Chris, who was an opioid addict, decided to go to rehab. But he needed to detoxify first, to get clean and sober. An inpatient program turned him down. "Multiple counselors told me that insurance companies don't want to spend the money on inpatient treatment unless you've failed at outpatient," Chris told the *Buffalo News*. He fought the insurance company (it's illegal for insurance companies to deny coverage) and was finally able to get into an inpatient facility.

Inpatient care is expensive, costing as much as $30,000 a month if you don't have insurance. It can last up to six months. Outpatient care is much cheaper. For their part, insurance companies seem to push for less expensive treatment options. Experts say individuals with strong expectations that inpatient will work for them appear to do much better than those who seek outpatient care.

first withdrawal experience was a physical and psychological nightmare. He became depressed, anxious and could not function. "I felt lonely and hopeless, just in the disease," he told a reporter. "But then going through withdrawal by myself in a motel room in Mexico was just a feeling of emptiness and despair. I had . . . runny eyes, runny nose, diarrhea, dehydration, complete lack of appetite, overwhelming nausea, pain in every part of my body."

METHADONE

Methadone is a derivative of opium that was first synthesized by German scientists in the 1930s; contrary to rumor, it was not put into production until after the World War II. In the early 1960s, doctors began administering methadone to help those addicted to opiates kick the habit.

Methadone has been used to ease opioid withdrawal symptoms for decades. A nurse hands a cup of methadone to a patient at a clinic in 1971.

The drug is available in pill or oral solution, and it works like morphine. Methadone blocks the receptors in the brain that are affected by opioids such as OxyContin and heroin, enabling users to experience a more gradual detox process rather than a more extreme and painful withdrawal process. When taken at the right dose, methadone eliminates the physical withdrawal symptoms and the mental cravings that are often associated with relapse, without creating the sense of euphoria associated with other opioids.

The effects of methadone last 24 to 36 hours, so most patients benefit from a single daily dose. Some methadone patients might feel anxious after taking the drug. They might become weak or drowsy. Some will lose their appetite or become constipated. Many patients find they have to take methadone for two to three years, while some only need the drug for several months.

If used correctly, methadone is an effective tool. However, the drug can be abused. According to the CDC, about 5,000 people die every year after overdosing on methadone. In fact, methadone accounts for about 30 percent of all deaths attributable to prescription painkillers. Most of the deaths can be linked to the illegal use and sale of methadone. Dealers often wait outside methadone clinics in an attempt to sell more heroin or opioid pills.

Some addicts switch from illicit opioids to methadone as a way to reduce the medical risks and criminal behavior associated with their drug abuse. Those who switch to methadone are less likely to commit crimes, or to contract HIV or hepatitis.

BUPRENORPHINE

Sarah Beach was a heroin user who had hit rock bottom. Within a year, she had lost her marriage, her home, her baby, her dog, and "every scrap of my self-respect." When she entered treatment, a doctor at the University of

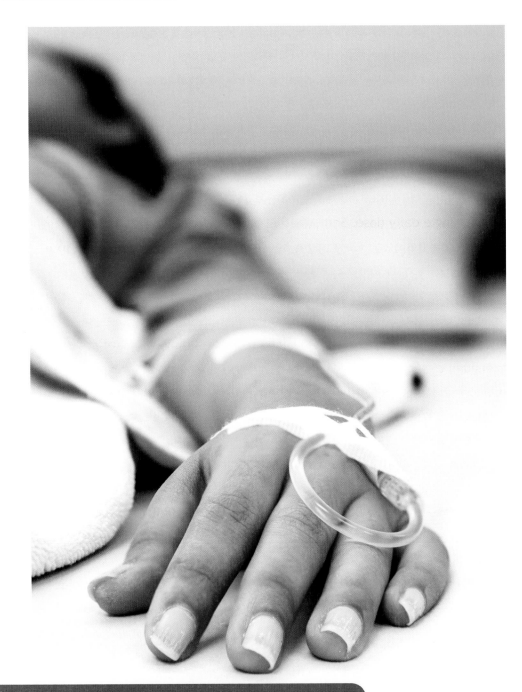

If someone has been using opioids regularly for a long time, the withdrawal symptoms can be dangerous. It is better to detox under medical supervision.

California at Berkeley was treating opioid addicts with a new drug, Suboxone. The main ingredient in Suboxone is a drug called buprenorphine. Approved in 2002, buprenorphine is an opioid-based medication that relieves cravings without producing the usual side effects. The drug can be taken orally.

The doctor told Sarah that because she was a heavy heroin user, she'd have to be in withdrawal for 72 hours before the first dose of Suboxone could be administered. "Then we'll have you come in here first thing the morning after, because you're going to be pretty unhappy at that point. And we'll get you induced [with Suboxone]. Within a few hours, I promise, you will feel much better. Not high—better than high. You'll feel normal," the doctor said.

The drug binds with the opiate receptors on brain cells, blocking other opiate molecules from binding with the receptor. Buprenorphine binds imperfectly with the receptors, which results in a limited opiate effect that is enough to stop withdrawal, but not enough for a person to experience a euphoric high. In its pure state, buprenorphine can be addictive, especially if injected. But Suboxone contains another drug called naloxone, which reduces that effect.

Sarah tried it. It worked. "My body was still and calm," she said. "The feeling of bugs crawling in and out of my skin vanished. My stomach settled and my head stopped whirling. . . . I noticed for the first time that it was a sunny day. The sunlight felt amazing on my face. Tears came to my eyes, but I laughed."

That was 10 years ago. Sarah hasn't used heroin or any other opioids since.

NARCAN

Narcan is a prescription medication that reverses an opioid overdose. It is not addictive, and addicts cannot use it to get high. Here's how Narcan

GOOD SAMARITANS

Twenty-two states and the District of Columbia have adopted so-called Good Samaritan laws, which protect anyone who calls 911 to report that someone is in need of Narcan. These laws provide immunity to the callers, so they do not have to worry about being arrested for using drugs. There is also a big push to allow first responders to administer Narcan.

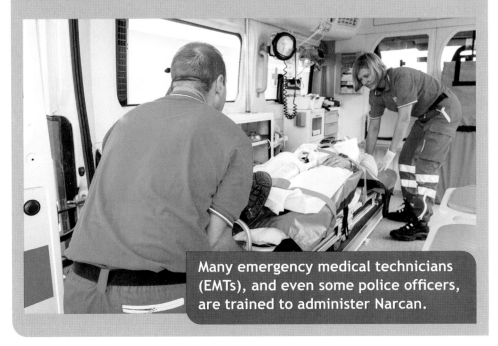

Many emergency medical technicians (EMTs), and even some police officers, are trained to administer Narcan.

works: a person overdoses when the drugs flood the receptor cells in the brain. When that happens, a person's breathing slows and can eventually stop. Narcan reverses the overdose by knocking the opioids off the receptor sites for a brief time, allowing a person to breathe normally again.

In 2013, 43,982 people died by overdosing on various drugs. Thirty-seven percent of those deaths, or 16,235, were related to opioid painkillers. Many states are now making Narcan kits available to laypersons to cut back on the number of overdose deaths. From 1996 through June

2014, Narcan kits were made available to more than 150,000 laypersons, resulting in the reversal of 26,463 overdoses.

CHANGING THE ADDICT'S MINDSET

Once an addict's body becomes less dependent on the drugs, the time has come to heal their minds. Changing the way a person thinks and behaves is essential for a good outcome. Most therapists say opioid addiction is a pattern of learned responses, mostly of reward and punishment. The cornerstone of good behavioral treatment is then to help the addict learn to identify any thoughts or situations that tempt them to use. The patient then has to find a way to avoid these temptations, while also considering what would happen if they use again. They learn stress management techniques, relaxation methods, and better problem-solving skills.

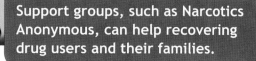

Support groups, such as Narcotics Anonymous, can help recovering drug users and their families.

A number of different types of therapies are available for those struggling with opioid addiction, including group therapy, in which other addicts share their experiences and concerns. By connecting with others in group therapy, an addict can begin to feel less helpless. The group also provides emotional support. Addicts can also go through individual psychotherapy to identify patterns of triggers that lead to drug use, learn coping skills, and replace their substance use with positive and healthy activities. Individual therapy can also help treat any underlying psychiatric symptoms and disorders.

BELL COUNTY FIGHTS BACK

Back in Bell County, the fight against opioid abuse has been an uphill struggle. As the drug crisis has increased, the money for treatment has decreased. But county residents have fought back. They funded Operation UNITE to battle drug abuse in southeastern Kentucky. A not-for-profit group, Operation UNITE uses a multifaceted approach to dealing with the community's drug crisis, including law enforcement investigations, treatment, and family support. When it lost almost half its funding in 2008–2009, the community banded together, raising enough cash so one of the counselors could stay on the job.

The group has tried to get the most vulnerable into treatment, while increasing recreational activities for youths. Moreover, local faith-based groups began to form support groups and other programs to help addicts and their families. Even the court system has allowed convicted addicts a chance at rehabilitation instead of going to jail. They must be drug-tested each week, go to school, and get a job, among other things. "We're No. 1 in the state now [in opiate abuse]," Cathy Woolum, who helped start Operation UNITE, told the *Louisville Courier*. "But where would we be if we didn't have these efforts going on here?"

TEXT-DEPENDENT QUESTIONS

1. How does methadone work, and why do doctors prescribe it to opioid abusers seeking treatment?
2. Why do insurance companies favor outpatient care over inpatient care?
3. What are the two main ingredients in Suboxone?

RESEARCH PROJECT

Get permission to visit a drug treatment facility in your community. Ask to interview a person going through treatment or a drug counselor. For those seeking treatment, ask specific questions about their lives before they entered treatment. Ask specific questions about their experiences undergoing treatment. If you can, record the interview and share it with your classmates. If not, take notes, and then write a story describing the interview.

If you interview a drug counselor, ask specific questions about what types of treatments are available. Did they go to treatment themselves? How do most people respond to treatment? What are the psychological and physical effects of drug treatment?

FURTHER READING

BOOKS AND ARTICLES

Adams, Taite. *Opiate Addiction: The Painkiller Addiction Epidemic, Heroin Addiction and the Way Out*. 3rd ed. St. Petersburg, FL: Rapid Response Press, 2015.

Hodgson, Barbara. *In the Arms of Morpheus: The Tragic History of Laudanum, Morphine, and Patent Medicines*. Buffalo, NY: Firefly Books, 2001.

Martin, Steven. *Opium Fiend: A 21st Century Slave to a 19th Century Addiction*. New York: Villard Books, 2012.

Pinksy, Drew, and Marvin D. Seppala. *When Painkillers Become Dangerous: What Everyone Needs to Know about OxyContin and Other Prescription Drugs*. Center City, MN: Hazelden Foundation, 2004.

ONLINE

Foundation for a Drug Free World. "The Truth about Heroin." http://www.drugfreeworld.org/drugfacts/heroin.html.

National Institute on Drug Abuse. "Treating Addiction to Prescription Opioids." http://www.drugabuse.gov/publications/research-reports/prescription-drugs/treating-prescription-drug-addiction/treating-addiction-to-prescription-opio.

Public Broadcasting Service. The Opium Kings. http://www.pbs.org/wgbh/pages/frontline/shows/heroin/.

EDUCATIONAL VIDEOS

Access these videos with your smartphone or use the URLs below to find them online.

 "What Makes Heroin So Deadly?," D News (a YouTube channel devoted to "mind-bending" facts). "What makes heroin more deadly than other drugs?" https://youtu.be/kSX6Z_k__Cc

 "OxyContin—Time Bomb," CBC News. "Canada has recorded the second-highest number of prescription opioid painkiller addictions and the world's second-highest death rate from overdoses." https://youtu.be/iNOHAJs9dBY

 "Heroin Epidemic in America," ABC News. "129 people die from drug overdoses every day, the majority from heroin and painkillers, more than guns and car accidents." https://youtu.be/xdnU7L4DjtI

 "CDC Issues New Guidelines." NBC News. "The CDC has issued its first federal guidelines on how to prescribe powerful opiate painkillers in an attempt to combat the addiction epidemic." https://youtu.be/0LMkA3N8ABg

 "Coming Back from the Dead with Naloxone," CNN. "Sanjay Gupta investigates if Naloxone, a drug that can reverse an overdose, can also help end the overdose epidemic." https://youtu.be/oWopsRaeY6M

SERIES GLOSSARY

abstention: actively choosing to not do something.

acute: something that is intense but lasts a short time.

alienation: a sense of isolation or detachment from a larger group.

alleviate: to lessen or relieve.

binge: doing something to excess.

carcinogenic: something that causes cancer.

chronic: ongoing or recurring.

cognitive: having to do with thought.

compulsion: a desire that is very hard or even impossible to resist.

controlled substance: a drug that is regulated by the government.

coping mechanism: a behavior a person learns or develops in order to manage stress.

craving: a very strong desire for something.

decriminalized: something that is not technically legal but is no longer subject to prosecution.

depressant: a substance that slows particular bodily functions.

detoxify: to remove toxic substances (such as drugs or alcohol) from the body.

ecosystem: a community of living things interacting with their environment.

environment: one's physical, cultural, and social surroundings.

genes: units of inheritance that are passed from parent to child and contain information about specific traits and characteristics.

hallucinate: seeing things that aren't there.

hyperconscious: to be intensely aware of something.

illicit: illegal; forbidden by law or cultural custom.

inhibit: to limit or hold back.

interfamilial: between and among members of a family.

metabolize: the ability of a living organism to chemically change compounds.

neurotransmitter: a chemical substance in the brain.

paraphernalia: the equipment used for producing or ingesting drugs, such as pipes or syringes.

physiological: relating to the way an organism functions.

placebo: a medication that has no physical effect and is used to test whether new drugs actually work.

predisposition: to be more inclined or likely to do something.

prohibition: when something is forbidden by law.

recidivism: a falling back into past behaviors, especially criminal ones.

recreation: something done for fun or enjoyment.

risk factors: behaviors, traits, or influences that make a person vulnerable to something.

sobriety: the state of refraining from alcohol or drugs.

social learning: a way that people learn behaviors by watching other people.

stimulant: a class of drug that speeds up bodily functions.

stressor: any event, thought, experience, or biological or chemical function that causes a person to feel stress.

synthetic: made by people, often to replicate something that occurs in nature.

tolerance: the state of needing more of a particular substance to achieve the same effect.

traffic: to illegally transport people, drugs, or weapons to sell throughout the world.

withdrawal: the physical and psychological effects that occur when a person with a use disorder suddenly stops using substances.

INDEX

ABOUT THE AUTHOR

John Perritano is an award-winning journalist, writer, and editor from Southbury CT., who has written numerous articles and books on a variety of subjects including science, sports, history, and culture for such publishers as Mason Crest, National Geographic, Scholastic and Time/Life. His articles have appeared on Discovery.com, Popular Mechanics.com and other magazines and Web sites. He holds a Master's Degree in American History from Western Connecticut State University.

ABOUT THE ADVISOR

Sara Becker, Ph.D. is a clinical researcher and licensed clinical psychologist specializing in the treatment of adolescents with substance use disorders. She is an Assistant Professor (Research) in the Center for Alcohol and Addictions Studies at the Brown School of Public Health and the Evaluation Director of the New England Addiction Technology Transfer Center. Dr. Becker received her Ph.D. in Clinical Psychology from Duke University and completed her clinical residency at Harvard Medical School's McLean Hospital. She joined the Center for Alcohol and Addictions Studies as a postdoctoral fellow and transitioned to the faculty in 2011. Dr. Becker directs a program of research funded by the National Institute on Drug Abuse that explores novel ways to improve the treatment of adolescents with substance use disorders. She has authored over 30 peer-reviewed publications and book chapters and serves on the Editorial Board of the *Journal of Substance Abuse Treatment*.

PHOTO CREDITS